Woman's SHAPE

PASTOR EBUA BUAM

authorHOUSE

AuthorHouse™
1663 Liberty Drive
Bloomington, IN 47403
www.authorhouse.com
Phone: 1 (800) 839-8640

Published by AuthorHouse 11/25/2015

ISBN: 978-1-5049-6289-6 (sc)
ISBN: 978-1-5049-6288-9 (e)

Print information available on the last page.

This book is printed on acid-free paper.

KJV
Scripture quotations marked KJV are from the Holy Bible, King James Version (Authorized Version). First published in 1611. Quoted from the KJV Classic Reference Bible, Copyright © 1983 by The Zondervan Corporation.

NIV.
Scripture quotations marked NIV are taken from the Holy Bible, New International Version®. NIV®. Copyright © 1973, 1978, 1984 by International Bible Society. Used by permission of Zondervan. All rights reserved. [Biblica]

CONTENTS

Dedication ix

Acknowledgement xi

Introduction xiii

Chapter 1   Man's Divine Task 1

Chapter 2   The Woman's Divine Shape 10

Chapter 3   Wisdom For Building And Destroying The Home
             (Proverb 24:3A) 25

Chapter 4   Understanding For Establishment
             (Proverb 24:3B) 34

Chapter 5   Knowledge For Beauty 42

Conclusion 55

References 57

*By wisdom a house is built, and through understanding
it is established; through knowledge its rooms are filled
with rare and beautiful treasures." Proverbs 24:3-4*

*"The wise woman builds her home but with her own hands
the foolish one tears hers down" Proverbs 14:1*

DEDICATION

DEDICATED TO OUR PRECIOUS LORD "CHRIST JESUS" WHO SHED HIS BLOOD SO THAT WE MIGHT TRACE OUR WAY BACK TO THE FATHER.

ACKNOWLEDGEMENT

First of all I will like to thank God Almighty for having made everything possible by giving me the strength and courage to do this work.

I express my deep sense of gratitude and indebtedness to my husband (Rev. Jerome Ebua) who, like a spiritual mentor and friend has always guided, encouraged and motivated me all along while writing this book.

My hearty thanks go to my parents Mr and Mrs Buam who brought us up in the ways of the Lord especially my Dad who let my mom stay abroad for over five months to give me a helping hand with the children so that I could have time enough to focus on the work, and to my mom as well for the time she dedicated in caring for my home and kids while I was busy with the ministry.

I feel deeply indebted to the following people for taking out time to proof read and edit this piece of work despite their busy schedule:

My dearest big sister "Anne-marie Buam" who did not only proof read but came to assist my mom with the kids during the peak of this work.

To Br Eric Ayum who despite the loss of his dad, did not hesitate to assist when I needed his help.

To Sr LIA. (Lord is Able) for her readiness and kind heart.

To my daughter and friend Jemimah, who has always been so responsible and encouraging especially during moments when things seemed not to be moving on well, she stood by me, showing love and care to her younger brother Jerome jr.

Pastor Ebua Buam

I am further grateful to all my family members as well as my friends for their support. Without you it would be very difficult to overcome all the challenges. I cannot say thanks enough

The completion of this book could not have been possible without the participation and assistance of so many people whose names may not all be enumerated. Your contributions are sincerely appreciated and gratefully acknowledged.

God richly bless you all

INTRODUCTION

It is virtually impossible to talk about the woman without mentioning the man since the woman came into existence as a result of man's lack of companionship. **"Woman's Shape"** is a divinely inspired book with the intention of responding to several questions like;

Why was the woman created?

What is her position or her place in creation?

What can she do to fulfil her divine role?

God created and placed man in the Garden of Eden for the unique purpose of worshiping him through the assignment he, God, gave man to dominate, work, multiply and care for the garden. After man had seen and named all the other creatures God created to be with him in the garden, there was still a void which none of the animals could fill, and God who always knows what our needs are and what is most suitable for us brought the woman into the scene, thus making a perfect match for the man. In this introductory part and chapter one, we shall be expounding on the divine position of Man in the garden, then we shall move on to the subsequent chapters which reveal how the woman came into the scene through creation, and detail the purpose of the woman, (The woman's shape) thus, answering the many questions which have so often been asked.

"Woman's Shape" is a handbook for every woman as it not only clearly defines the role of the woman in the garden, but equally reveals the instruments and wisdom that she can practically use to either build or destroy her home. It also helps women to understand various personalities in their environment for a better approach and knowledge in some

fundamental aspects of their home and surroundings in order for it to be managed properly and effectively and above all to be women according to God's plans.

THE DIVINE POSITION OF MAN IN THE GARDEN *Genesis 2:8-10*

"Now the lord God had planted a garden in the east, in Eden; and there he put the man he had formed. And the lord God made all kinds of trees grow out of the ground – trees that were pleasing to the eye and good for food. In the middle of the garden were the tree of life and the tree of the knowledge of good and evil. A river watering the garden flowed from Eden; from there it was separated into four headwaters"

The garden is the divine location for man. God prepared and equipped it with everything needed for him to accomplish his mission here on earth. It is a place of regular work and ample return. Man is master in the garden. His orders and authority can be fully implemented with great achievement in this divine position. He did not need to strain to get water for his products as water flowed freely and naturally from Eden to water all his efforts for a great yield

Gen 2:10b "A river watering the garden flowed from Eden; from there it was separated into four headwaters".

Life in the garden today points to life in Christ Jesus. Jesus is our divine location. It is God's will that all should repent and come to Jesus where life is found. On the other hand, water symbolizes the Holy Spirit in that just as water flowed from Eden watering the garden, so too is the Holy Spirit given to those who are in Christ for effective service when they take their position in him. When we work through his leading, our efforts are never in vain. Working with the Holy Spirit will always result in a great yield. The Holy Spirit equips us with necessary gifts, talents, Wisdom, understanding, Knowledge and all kinds of skills needed for us to accomplish our divine mandate.

I Cor. 12:4-11 *"there are different kinds of gifts, but the same Spirit distributes them. There are different kinds of service, but the same Lord. There are different kinds of working, but in all of them and in everyone it is the same God at work". Now to each one the manifestation of the Spirit is given for the common good. ⁸ To one there is given through the Spirit a message of wisdom, to another a message of knowledge by means of the same Spirit, ⁹ to another faith by the same Spirit, to another gifts of healing by that one Spirit, ¹⁰ to another miraculous powers, to another prophecy, to another distinguishing between spirits, to another speaking in different kinds of tongues,[a] and to still another the interpretation of tongues.[b] ¹¹ All these are the work of one and the same Spirit, and he distributes them to each one, just as he determines*

The Spirit comes to help us realise our mission here on earth. Jesus promises to send the Holy Spirit to those who love him to help them fulfill this divine task

""Whoever believes in me, as Scripture has said, rivers of living water will flow from within them." ³⁹ by this he meant the Spirit, whom those who believed in him were later to receive. Up to that time the Spirit had not been given, since Jesus had not yet been glorified". John 7:38-39

John 14:15-26. Water speaks of life, greenness, freshness. Etc. When we depend on the Lord, we are always renewed. Our ideas are always fresh and dryness or barrenness has no place in our lives. In the above scripture verse

39b reads *"Up to that time, the Spirit had not been given since Jesus had not yet been glorified".*

Jesus must accomplish his mission as a savior in our lives before we can start enjoying the empowerment of the Holy Spirit. We must give our lives to Christ and become born again for Jesus to be glorified. When we are at our divine location, we glorify Jesus. Jesus is our divine location and it is through this that he can be connected to us by his Spirit to equip us for our divine assignment.

Chapter 1

MAN'S DIVINE TASK

Gen. 2"15 The LORD God took the man and put him in the Garden of Eden to work it and take care of it. ¹⁶ And the LORD God commanded the man, "You are free to eat from any tree in the garden; ¹⁷ but you must not eat from the tree of the knowledge of good and evil, for when you eat from it you will certainly die."

"Then God said, "Let us make man in our image, in our likeness, and let them rule over the fish of the sea and the birds of the air, over the livestock, over all the earth, and over all the creatures that move along the ground." So God created man in his own image, in the image of God he created him male and female he created them. God blessed them and said to them, "Be fruitful and increase in number; fill the earth and subdue it. Rule over the fish of the sea and the birds of the air and over every living creature that moves on the ground." Gen. 1: 26-28

Essentially, *Gen 2* is fulfilled before *Gen 1: 28*. In *Gen 1:28*, God had already made the woman out of the man. It was a kind of summary of God's creation. *Genesis 2* gives details of the beginning of creation, and in *verse 15*, only the male man was given instructions patterning to the garden as God's representative. The woman later appears in the scene in *verse 22.* Man's tasks in the garden were as follow;

I.   **To rule – Genesis 1:26:** God gave man a superior spirit in creating him in God's own image and likeness which gave him authority that was to psychologically, emotionally and spiritually influence all other creatures to submit to his authority. This is the reason why by nature, man wants to dominate at all times. Man always wants to be in a place of authority and this is because God made him a superior being. God wanted to see himself through man as his representative in ruling and this goes as far as pleasing and glorifying God.

II. **Work and Care for the garden – Gen. 2:15**: God never gave man the impression that he was to provide everything for him from heaven. He gave man all he needed to make life easy in the garden but man had to work and care for it and in return eat of its produces with the exception of the forbidden tree. The bible says

"All hard work brings a profit but mere talk leads only to poverty" Prov. 14:23.

No one in the garden should be idle. There is a common English adage that "an idle mind is the devil's workshop." God expects us to be busy with work so as to accomplish the assignment he created us for.

III. **To multiply**: This indicates fruitfulness. Multiplication comes as a result of hard work. Just like we have already said above, "all hard work brings a profit". There's no hard work that is in vain especially for those who in Christ Jesus are functioning according to their divine shape. Exercising someone else's ministry that does not match our design does not bring much yield and make us feel unfulfilled. God has given every single individual here on earth talents and when we come under the shelter of Jesus, he adds unto these talents spiritual gifts that equip us more for effective ministry. Statistically, it is proven that each single person has about five hundred talents or more. God gives us tasks according to the talents we have; to some he gives much and to others he gives little and expects every person to be fruitful and multiply that which he gives him/her. *Matt. 25:24-30.* Our reward will depend on what we make of that which he gives us. *Matt. 25:19-30*

[14] "For it will be like a man going on a journey, who called his servant and entrusted to them his property. [15] To one he gave five talents, to another two, to another one, to each according to

his ability. Then he went away. ¹⁶ He who had received the five talents went at once and traded with them, and he made five talents more. ¹⁷ So also he who had the two talents made two talents more. ¹⁸ But he who had received the one talent went and dug in the ground and hid his master's money. ¹⁹ Now after a long time the master of those servants came and settled accounts with them.

²⁰ And he who had received the five talents came forward, bringing five talents more, saying, 'Master, you delivered to me five talents; here I have made five talents more.' ²¹ His master said to him, 'Well done, good and faithful servant you have been faithful over a little; I will set you over much. Enter into the joy of your master.' ²² And he also who had the two talents came forward, saying, 'Master, you delivered to me two talents; here I have made two talents more.' ²³ His master said to him, 'Well done, good and faithful servant. You have been faithful over a little; I will set you over much. Enter into the joy of your master.' ²⁴ He also who had received the one talent came forward, saying, 'Master, I knew you to be a hard man, reaping where you did not sow, and gathering where you scattered no seed, ²⁵ so I was afraid, and I went and hid your talent in the ground. Here you have what is yours.' ²⁶ But his master answered him, 'you wicked and slothful servant! You knew that I reap where I have not sown and gather where I scattered no seed? ²⁷ Then you ought to have invested my money with the bankers, and at my coming I should have received what was my own with interest. ²⁸ So take the talent from him and give it to him who has the ten talents. ²⁹ For to everyone who has will more be given, and he will have an abundance. But from the one who has not, even what he has will be taken away. ³⁰ And cast the worthless servant into the outer darkness. In that place there will be weeping and gnashing of teeth.'

The parable of the talents gives us a clear idea of what God expects us to do here on earth. God gives talents as it pleases him. To some he gives much and to some little yet we are not to question him but to be grateful and multiply even the little he gives us. We should not expect to always do things better than others. God might have given others more than he gave us. All he needs to see is our faithfulness in the little he gave us and then more will be added to that little as we see from the above scriptures.

We also read from *verse 28-30* the result of not appreciating God and multiplying our talents. Using our talents is the main purpose why we're here on earth and this is why it is a very vital area of concern as Christians to know what talents God has given us and to develop and start multiplying while serving Him in them through the Holy Spirit.

2. CONDITION FOR MAN TO FULFILL HIS DIVINE TASK

a.   The condition of work

As we already said, God never gave man the impression that he will provide everything for him from heaven but instead gave him an environment suitable enough for him to execute his divine task. The work principle still applies today and even does so on a more serious note. As we read in *proverb 14:23.* Man is supposed to be busy in the garden as a good representative of his creator. Scripture records that God worked for six days and rested on the seventh. **Gen 1:31 and Gen. 2:2.** If man is representing God here on earth, he ought to replicate him as well. The father and Son are always busy with work.

(John 5:17) "My Father is always at his work to this very day, and I, too, am working."

God considers the work principle very seriously so much so that the apostle Paul in one of his writings to the Thessalonians gives a rule that man should not eat if he doesn't work.

"For even when we were with you, we gave you this rule: 'If a man will not work, he shall not eat.'" 2Thess.3:10

We ought to take seriously the work that puts our daily bread on the table. Idleness is a sin. It should be noted here that there's a difference between idleness and rest. God rested and for us to be balanced, we ought to work and rest. Idleness is excessive rest. Paul goes even further to say believers should avoid idle brethren in the name of the Lord.

"In the name of the Lord Jesus Christ, we command you, brothers and sisters, to keep away from every believer who is idle and disruptive and does not live according to the teaching you received from us. (2 Thessalonians 3:6)

b. The condition of the forbidden tree

""And the Lord God commanded man saying; of every tree of the garden you may freely eat : but of the tree of the knowledge of good and evil you shall not eat, for in the day that you eat of it you shall surely die." (Gen 2: 16 – 17)

Man was not to eat from the forbidden tree; the forbidden tree can represent much in our present dispensation. Below, we shall outline some of the aspects that can represent the forbidden tree in our Christian lives in today's context. The Lord told man that the day he eats of the forbidden tree he shall surely die. Death here was metaphorical as it was not physical but spiritual. It simply means losing God's presence and in the absence of God's presence, there is toiling and tilling.

❖ *Sin: Isaiah 59:1-3*

"Surely the arm of the Lord is not too short to save, nor his ear too dull to hear. <u>But your iniquities have separated you from your God, your sins have hidden his face form you, so that he will not hear.</u> For your hands are stained with blood, your fingers with guilt, your lips have spoken lies, and your tongue mutters wicked things"

Sin is one of the forbidden fruits. It is one of the things that separates us from God or takes us out of the garden. Sin simply means violating God's Law. Sin is anything that we do or do not do that grieves the Spirit of God within us. When man violated God's law in the Garden of Eden by eating the forbidden fruit, God sent him out of the garden. When we sin and violate God's Law, we lose our authority in the garden and the absence of this authority is replaced by fear, the desire to do God's purpose is replaced by carnality. We start following the world's pattern and we are separated from God

Romans 8:5-8

"Those who live according to the sinful nature have their minds set on what that nature desires; but those who live in accordance with the Spirit have their minds set on what the Spirit desires. The mind of sinful man is death, but the mind controlled by the Spirit is life and peace; the sinful mind is hostile to God. It does not submit to God's law, the sinful nature cannot please God"

Without God's presence, how can we enter our divine purpose and operate befittingly in a way that will glorify him? Many in the world are gifted with talents and skills but the glory is not given to God and it is difficult for such to feel fulfilled because they cannot reach their full potentials in the absence of the empowerment of the Holy Spirit. When we are out of Christ, we no longer live a Spirit led life but a carnally minded one, and therefore, our minds are set on what that sinful nature desires, **'worldliness'**.

❖ *Operating in the wrong ministry:* Eating the forbidden fruit can equally mean operating in a ministry that is not the one God designed for us. Because of selfishness, futile competition, imitation and carnal desires, people start operating ministries which are not God inspired or spirit led. That is why very little or no returns are experienced. We put in much money and efforts and yet the yield is so insignificant. Our toiling and tilling begins when we get involved in ministries or operations that we were not shaped for. Not everybody can do business, be a pastor or even become an artist. Etc. If every human being were to operate according to his/her divine shape, there would be little or no jealousy, envy, killing, aimless competition. Etc. All these are caused by a lack of fulfilment. Each person is created for a precise task here on earth. Never do what was not intended for you else, you won't excel or feel fulfilled. Putting a square peck in a round hold does not work nor does using a sewing machine as a blender work either.

When man sinned by eating the fruit from the forbidden tree, God sent him out of the garden. He was no longer in his divine location and therefore could not exercise what God created him for. As a result, his suffering began. He had to toil and till in order to gather little; life out of the garden is that of toiling and tilling. Man lost all the advantages he had. It was no longer regular work but hard work. He lost his authority. We thank God for Jesus Christ through whom we have regained our access to the garden. Jesus is the light in our darkness. When we receive him in to our lives, his light takes off the veil of darkness and opens up our understanding as we live a consecrated life and this light shines the way through the path or purpose which he prearranged for us.

Paul in **Romans chapter 8** talks about the canal minded Christian; there are many who claim to be in Christ and yet live according to the desires of the flesh by following their carnal nature. It is impossible for such to please God or experience the free peaceful and prosperous life in the garden. God is not a man to lie. His word remains the absolute truth man can believe in. It is not possible to live in the garden and do the rightful chore God designed for us and yet live a life of permanent poverty. God, I believe can let his children go through a situation of lack for a time but not permanently throughout their entire lives. The desert is a passage into the promise land and not a home. We cannot be serving a great God or claim that our father is rich and yet live in perpetual poverty. This doesn't make any sense nor does it bring honor unto the one whom we claim to be our father.

a) The condition of the male man leading

In this great mission that God gave man in the garden, man was to do this task alone. After God had finished, he realized man was lonely so he had to make a woman to be his companion or help,

Gen 2:18.

"The Lord God said, "It is not good for the man to be alone. I will make a helper suitable for him."

In the garden, the male man essentially was the person according to God's word who was to do the task. The woman came last of all God's creatures after man's assignment had been given. She was the finished work of man and that is why women most often appear to be more polished than men. This doesn't mean there are particular ministries the woman cannot operate in. Remember in the book of **Joel 2:29** God says he will pour out his spirit on both men and women in the later days. The woman is only physically weak but spiritually, God can use her in any area that pleases him and this will obviously come to compliment her husband in the area of his want. One of the primary duties of a Christian woman is to inquire of her husband what God is laying in his heart to accomplish here on earth. She ought to equally ask the lord in prayers the purpose for which he brought her and her husband together, and if they are doing the right thing and on the right track. God the creator created Adam and placed him in the garden and Eve his wife was created as a helper to help him in fulfilling this assignment. Every person is created for a particular purpose and by not asking God to reveal it to us and direct us towards it simply means we have decided to take our lives and destinies into our hands. We have decided to lead our lives, thereby taking the place of God the potter who shaped us for a particular reason. We have ripped God of his glory.

The bible declares in **Romans 19:21b, Isaiah 45:9-1 that** God is the potter and we are the clay and the potter has authority over the clay. The clay has no right whatsoever to question the potter why he made him for a particular use. If you indulge in an activity or ministry that is not divinely inspired, this simply and indirectly means you do not appreciate God the potter for the way he has molded you or in other words, his purpose for creating you.

Romans 19:21b

""Shall what is formed say to him who formed it, 'why did you make me like this? '"Does not the potter have the right to make out of the same lump of clay some pottery for noble purposes and some for common use?

Only the potter knows the purpose for which he designs the clay and he shapes the clay according to that purpose and therefore only him can clearly say the purpose of the particular clay and how it functions.

Isaiah 45:9-11

"Woe to him who quarrels with his Maker, to him who is but a potsherd among the potsherds on the ground. Does the clay say to the potter, 'what are you making?' Does your work say, 'He has no hands? Woe to him who says to his father, 'what have you begotten?' or to his mother, 'What have you brought to birth? This is what the Lord says – the Holy One of Israel, and its Maker: Concerning things to come, do you question me about my children, or give me orders about the work of my hands?"

Jeremiah 1:4-7

"The word of the Lord came to me, saying, "Before I formed you in the womb I knew you, before you were born I set you apart; I appointed you as a prophet to the nations "Ah, Sovereign Lord," I said, "I do not know how to speak, I am only a child" But the Lord said to me,: Do not say I am only a child. You must go to everyone I send you to and say whatever I command you."

We should therefore be happy to be in the place where God wants us to be and do the things he shaped us to do, for therein hidden is our breakthrough and fulfillment. As we see in the book of Jeremiah, before we were ever born, God had a plan for us and he brought us into the world to accomplish that plan.

Chapter 2

THE WOMAN'S DIVINE SHAPE

By wisdom a house is built, and through understanding it is established; through knowledge its rooms are filled with rare and beautiful treasures."
Proverbs 24:3-4

The next four chapters are inspired from the above scripture; we shall be looking at the role of the woman in the garden as God had anticipated in creation. We shall also examine some of the instruments which can serve the woman to either destroy or build her home with biblical examples of some women in bible times. The emphasis in chapter four will be on the different kinds of personalities as well as approaches most appropriate for the various types that will serve as tools for the establishment of the woman in her home and her environment. Then we will continue to the fifth chapter which is essentially a practical one. Some examples of studies that are carried out at the Wisdom for women training centers will be given. In this chapter, we encourage women to visit our centers where most of the practical work is done.

As we have already seen in chapter one, the woman has the place of a helper in the garden. The garden here can mean "The home or Ministry". By implication, she occupies the second position of authority, for it was the man that was given the task to work and till and she was created to help the man. God placed the male man in this position and each time the woman tries to be in charge, it causes conflict. That is why the key into a man's heart is submission. This doesn't make her in any way the lesser man for she is merely in her *"**Divine shape**"*. This concept is elaborated more for a clearer understanding as we unfold it in the preceding paragraphs.

Take note that in *__Joel 2:29__*. Joel emphasizes that the Holy Spirit will be given to "both men and women." This text tells us that the Holy Spirit will pour His power into women equally and because the woman has the same outpouring of the Holy Spirit as the man, there is no limitation as to what God can use her to do. As a married woman, all it takes is to operate under the authority of her husband.

I. THE ROLE OF THE WOMAN IN THE GARDEN

Proverbs 14:1

"The wise woman builds her home but with her own hands the foolish one tears hers down"

A. As a wife- A helper: Genesis 2:18-20

> *"The Lord God said it is not good for the man to be alone. I will make a helper suitable for him. Now the lord God had formed out of the ground all the beasts of the field and all the birds of the air. He brought them to the man to see what he would name them, and whatever the man called each living creature, that was its name. So the man gave names to all the livestock, the birds of the air and all the beasts of the field. But for Adam, no suitable helper was found. So the lord God caused the man to fall into a deep sleep, and while he was sleeping, he took one of the man's ribs and closed up the place with flesh. The lord God made a woman from the rib he had taken out of the man, and he brought her to the man. The man said this is now bone of my bones, and flesh of my flesh. She shall be called woman for she was taken out of man".*

We notice as we read through Genesis Chapter two that the woman was the last of God's creation. God created the woman when everything in the garden was ready. What a red carpet position women occupy in creation. She comes in when all is complete. She is certainly specially prepared to

11

bring completeness in the man's life and ministry. Take note of the man's reaction when he suddenly woke up from his deep sleep and notices this special creature that immediately filled his emptiness and caused him to exclaim. **"This is now bone of my bones and flesh of my flesh"** He said <u>**"this is now"**</u> implying upon all the time he was with the other creatures, none was similar to him or made him to feel complete. The man was already busy working in the garden and just needed someone who will be a suitable companion and complete what he has begun. The help the bible mentions is not only physical for God has invested in the man the physical ability to do all sort of work and the man was already working successfully.

The help here is also moral and spiritual. God has invested a very strong intuition in the woman. The woman has a great and powerful ability to spur someone to do something. Help here does not imply the woman is inferior or lesser than the man. God himself is described as our help. In fact one of his names is Ebenezer which means the Lord is my help. One of Moses' sons is named Eliezer meaning "my God is my help". The Holy Spirit too is described in scriptures as our helper. This idea of the woman described as the helper cannot be measured. It is a red carpet and honourable position. It essentially makes her more or less indispensable to the man. She is gifted with a strong willpower, perseverance, patience, foresightedness etc. and when she commits to do a thing, she wholeheartedly puts all these qualities in place for it to actualize. This is what a man who will fulfil destiny requires.

With these great capabilities in her, she can be a great source of encouragement and motivation to her husband and children if she applies it in her **divine shape**. Eve saw the fruit, noticed that it was good for food, and pleasing to the eye and also desiring to be like God. She succeeded through her great ability to convince her physically strong husband who had been in the garden working and living in obedience long before she ever came.

Genesis 3:6-7

"When the woman saw that the fruit of the tree was good for food and pleasing to the eye, and also desirable for gaining wisdom, she took

some and ate it. She also gave some to her husband, who was with her, and he ate it".

Queen Esther through her great inner capacity took the risk of going into the palace being a foreigner and contested for the vacant post of the queen. She did not only end there, when the time of disaster was about to come upon her people, she equally risked her life by going into the king's inner court without being summoned by the king knowing fully well that she stands the risk of dying if the king does not extend the golden sceptre towards her. *Esther 4:11, 5:1-2.* We equally notice Jezebel, Ahab's wife who was so determined in doing evil by serving the god of her fore fathers (the Baal) and succeeded to induce her husband and the whole nation of Israel into the worship of this false god. What about Deborah, Jael, Delilah and many other women in the bible who reflect the strong capacity God has given to the woman?

God's original intention was that the woman will come in with her great capacity to encourage and motivate the man in tending and keeping the garden according to how he, God, had anticipated, but unfortunately, it was not the case with Eve. Women are special as they possess the power to build and to destroy *"Proverb 14:1"*. God's will for women is that they should build by filling the lapse in the man. They should fill that empty hole at the side of the man from where they were taken out, and encourage their husbands in doing that for which God created them. They should stand by them even when things seem not to be working out, for they have the ability. With the same power they took man out of the garden, they can use it to bring him back into the garden.

It is the woman's responsibility to take her husband back in to the garden if he is not yet in it. Preach to him not necessarily by words but through her life style of submission and the fear of God.

"Wives, in the same way submit yourselves to your own husbands so that, if any of them do not believe the word, they may be won over without words by the behaviour of their wives, ² when they see the purity and reverence of your lives" 1 peter 3:1-2

She was created to bear children. Let her first child be her husband. Nurture, teach and guide him with the word of God and the power to endure that is in her. Be his first pastor. God has given the woman the ability, which is why we realize in active life that some things men cannot endure the woman does. An example is the woman's tolerance with an unruly or disloyal husband or children. Most women endure and forgive such acts of their husbands and children, a thing most men cannot stand. The woman can win her husband over to the lord's side or bring him into the garden if she explores the capacity within her through patience, prayers, love, gentleness, meekness and hope in the lord etc., she has all these qualities within her.

The woman equally has the responsibility of making sure they are not eating the forbidden fruit while in the garden. That is to say they are not exercising the wrong ministry or activity. She should be able to know through her gift of discernment the purpose for which God called her husband, by being interested in what he likes doing; observing what he does best without much time and efforts; remind and encourage him of it at all times and help him remain focussed on it. She should be prompt at any time to support her husband in the area he needs support, take interest in his work and hobbies, talk over problems and be a good listener, study · the bible together with him, make time to have some fun together, be sympathetic and compassionate when necessary, keep peace and harmony in the house, show respect for him, encourage and support him where necessary. All the above are very supportive role the woman can play as a helper.

Some people have the stereotype idea that the woman's duty is to help her husband only in doing the household chores and caring for the children. What about husbands who prefer to cook their food, wash their clothes etc., will she insist on helping her husband only in those when he himself feels he does better than her? Jerome (my husband) does not feel helped when I cook or wash his clothes or even do household work. He prefers me to minister alongside with him beside my household duties, give him innovative and supportive ideas or boost him up with encouraging words when he's morally down. Ignoring the area of his need and concentrating on a stereotypical idea of help does not fill the gap. The woman was taken out of the man and when she comes into his life, she ought to fit into the hole from where she was removed. She ought to discern that hole or emptiness in her husband. These are the things the husband cannot do and then fill in the gap by doing the things he is unable to do. By so doing, she compliments him and this is what will make her husband miss her in her absence or feel her indispensability in his life. So know the specific area where your husband needs help and play your role as a help mate best.

B. As a mother (A child bearer)

"And Adam was not deceived but the woman being deceived, fell into transgression. Nevertheless she will be saved in childbearing if they continue in faith, love, and holiness with self-control". 1 Timothy 2:15

Childbearing is the "raison d'être" of the woman. The bible clearly says she can only be saved through childbearing. The notion of childbearing is not physical but mainly spiritual. Childbearing involves nurturing, teaching and guiding. In other words, the woman as a mother has the responsibility to nurture, teach and guide, and she can only be saved if she does these things in faith, in love, holiness and self-control. This simply means she has to be a model in faith by sharing and living her faith, be a model in showing love, a model in holy living and self-control. By doing these, she is childbearing as many will stand in the faith by her example. The woman needs to be a model for she has a strong inner power that can either influence those around her positively or negatively. Her first child to child bear is her husband and she ought to do these in faith, in love, holiness, self-control and I should add submission. She does this not only by words but by her life style and examples.

i. As a nurturer

"She opens her mouth with wisdom. And on her tongue is the law of kindness. She watches over the ways of her household and <u>does not eat the bread of idleness". Proverb 31:27</u>

To nurture means to promote the development of someone or a plant. Women by nature are nurturers. Within them, the Holy Spirit has established a nurturing spirit that will not allow them to push away their young but to nurse them and care for them. A pregnant woman for example shares her food and oxygen with her unborn baby. Her breasts gradually collect milk and in future become the place where her unborn baby will be nourished. In

15

her the baby feels complete as he eats from her, finds comfort, protection, love and intimacy.

In the above scriptures we notice that the wise woman watches over the ways of her household to make sure that they are balanced. As a nurturer, the woman ought to watch over her household (home, the church and surrounding) to make sure they are well nourished both spiritually and physically. This therefore implies that the woman should be a hard worker like the virtuous woman of proverb 31. Things are not like in those days when the woman concentrates only on household work and expects the man to give her everything she needs and also provides for the entire home.

The standard of life has become so high that the two need to put hands together for the family's comfort. For the family to be well nourished spiritually and physically, the mother needs to work hard in both aspects. To nourish her family spiritually, she ought to know the word of God herself by studying, meditating and reading the bible, she ought to be prayerful and discerning the will of God in situations so that the family or the church does not go astray. She has to be a physically hard working person so that her husband and children are well physically.

ii. As a teacher

"Listen, my son, to your father's instructions and do not forsake <u>your mother's teachings.</u> They will be a garland to grace your head and a chain to adorn your neck". Proverb 1:8-9

Although both parents have as responsibility to teach the children, it is the woman's divine shape and one of her primary roles. According to the above scriptures, the father gives instructions while the mother teaches. Instructors are generally characterized with giving orders. Once the order is given, they expect immediate execution. Instructors are generally impatient and will rage when an order is not executed. A teacher on the other hand is patient, teaches by example while hoping that things will change for the better.

Proverbs 10:1

A wise son brings joy to his father, <u>but a foolish son brings grief to his mother</u>.(NIV)

Proverbs 29:15

The rod and reproof give wisdom: <u>but a child left to himself bringeth his mother to shame.(kjv)</u>

Because it is one of the mother's elemental roles to teach the child, if the child is foolish or mislaid, he naturally brings grief or shame to her. In life generally, we notice that the good children are daddy's while the stubborn ones are mommy's. The father will naturally hold the mother accountable for a fault committed by the child. Instead of being angry, mothers should learn to take the challenge with their inner transforming power and be more determined than ever to teach their children and spend time praying for them.

What should the woman teach?

❖ *Teach Genesis 3:15.*

"And I will put enmity between you and the woman, and between your seed and her seed; He shall bruise your head, and you shall bruise his heel".

After the fall in the garden, the lord placed a curse on the devil. He said the woman's seed shall bruise the serpent's head. It is the woman's seed and not the man's. Bruising here simply means silencing and frustrating the devil's plan by not helping him accomplish his mission which is to kill, steal and destroy thereby abolishing God's salvific plan for humanity. It simply implies that any child born of a woman is a child of destiny; he is a bruiser of the devil's head be he illegitimate according to human standard. By God's standard, every child is legitimate. He is not a mistake for the lord permitted his coming into the world. It is the woman's role to teach the child this. The child is born for a particular purpose. The woman with the help of the Holy Spirit should seek to know the purpose for which this child came into the world and in that area teach the child. As already said in *Jeremiah 1:5* that before we ever came into the world, God had a well-defined purpose for creating us. The woman ought to guide and nurture the child in that light like Hannah did with Samuel. Make sure the child stays in that area as he grows up, and bruises the head of the serpent thereby fulfilling his destiny here on earth.

I have had the opportunity to pastor for several years and it is no news that some mothers discourage their children from some careers just because it is not on the popular side knowing fully well how their child is gifted in that particular area. By so doing, they're not helping the child in bruising the devil's head but instead help in eating the forbidden fruit. Mothers are there to discern the area of a child's giftedness and help in developing it, thereby bruising the head of the serpent.

❖ Teach good morals or behavioural ethics:

It is so embarrassing how some parents neglect their children's unruly behaviour. It is very common nowadays to see how children ignorantly do things which are not generally acceptable in the society. Sometimes parents don't even notice or they themselves are ignorant about these. It is obvious that each culture has their cultural dos and don'ts and therefore it is important for parents to take note about the society in which they are so as to better teach their children. It is not polite for example in most African cultures for the young to bypass an elderly person without greeting or greet an elder in a very casual manner, or lean behind an elder's seat while the elder is seating, intervene when parents discuss with someone or a friend, eat and abandon the table for parents to clear, call an elderly person by their name or even extend hands to greet an elderly person. All these are very poor moral standards in an African context which a mother who finds herself in such a society should seriously put an eye on and

correct otherwise the child will obviously bring shame to bear on her as the bible states

❖ **Teach life's principles:**

There are basic principles in life that the mother ought to teach the child about the consequences of their non-implementation. For example; to succeed, you must work hard. Or to be educated you must go to school.

I remember when my daughter (Jemimah) reached the age of going to school; I realized she was too fearful so I needed to prepare her. Since I knew she had often expressed the desire in owning her own plane in future, I told her the only way she could get into the airplane or even buy one for herself was to go to school, work hard in her studies and in future have the means to hire one for herself but if not she will have to get ready to become a roadside seller or beggar. This worked like miracle. Flying an airplane became the main drive for her studies at that time.

Teach your children basic life's principles for as we have seen from the above *scripture proverb 1:8-9*, these teachings will become garland to grace their heads and chains to adorn their necks. A garland is a wreath of flowers worn or hung as a decoration. Chains and flowers worn on the body are for beautifying. What will actually beautify a well taught child are not the physical chains or make-ups he/she wears but the teachings of the mother as he/she applies them.

iii. As a guide

"She opens her mouth with wisdom. And on her tongue is the law of kindness. <u>She watches over the ways of her household</u> and does not eat the bread of idleness". Proverb 31:27

A guide is someone who watches over to make sure everything is done correctly. As a guide therefore, the mother should watch closely over her child both spiritually and physically as he grows and learns about life. You should not forget the fact that your child interacts with other children from different backgrounds and different education at school, church, playgrounds etc. The mother should make out time to discuss with her child about his/her friends, teachers, aunties, uncles etc. and endeavour to do away with any ungodly teaching.

Once as I was discussing with my daughter about her day when she got home from school, she immediately asked me which church was the best. Surprised by her out of topic question, I threw it back at her asking which she thought was the best suspecting she must have been told something in school and she shouted out that "the Catholic Church is the first and the best." She went further to say there are beautiful pictures and images of all the saints and Jesus which we do not have in our church. I immediately told her no church is the best nor important but it is the relationship a church or an individual shares with the lord which matters. I went further to explain God's love towards man but how man instead of returning this love to the invisible God who should be worshipped in spirit and in truth, decided to make images which God had forbidden in his word, *Exodus 20:2-4*. I used this opportunity to read this scripture with her and many others and asked her if it is the inner or outer beauty that matters and she quickly said the inner. The mother should guide her child to make sure he/she grows balanced both spiritually and physically protecting him/her from anything that may come to destroy his/her values.

C. The woman as a minister of the gospel

The Christian woman is a minister of the gospel as we have seen above as one of her duty in childbearing. Being a minister of God does not automatically mean she stands on the pulpit to preach. In as much as she can preach from the pulpit, she can as well minister through her lifestyle. To effectively bear children through our lives in our present world, there are some obvious criteria. The woman minister of the Gospel is a woman of Integrity, Substance and a dynamic woman.

❖ **Woman of Integrity**

Integrity simply means having high moral principles

Hebrew 12:1

"Therefore, since we are surrounded by such a great cloud of witnesses, let us throw off everything that hinders and the sin that so easily

entangles, and let us run with perseverance the race marked out for us. Let us fix our eyes on Jesus, the author and perfecter of our faith".

As a woman of integrity, she should always be conscious of the fact that she is surrounded by a great cloud of witnesses, and being aware that her surrounding including the heavenly host is observing and noticing her character, she should always be conscious about keeping very high moral principles. She must not be known for example as a nagging woman, quarrelsome or always disputing with people, a debtor, cheat, gossip or being disrespectful because these are very poor and belittling morals which automatically denigrate her image and self-respect.

❖ **A woman of substance:** By a woman of substance, we simply mean a strong, solid and wealthy woman. We mean the modern woman who has not allowed herself to be boxed with personal or stereotypical ideas of those around her but a woman who has understood that God made her special and is free to be everything God has gifted her to be. A woman of substance does not allow the world to define her womanhood. She knows God's call and capacity to her life, obeys; explores and enjoys the opportunities set before her while being submissive to God, her husband and her pastor. *Hebrew 13:17.* She uses her God's given talents, strength and opportunities to create wealth.

She understands that the world is evolving and it is difficult for the man alone to sustain the home. She is conscious that the work of God does not only need spiritual support but financial and material support as well.

In our contemporary world, wealth is the icebreaker. Become wealthy and you will have countless opportunities to enter places, preach the gospel, and be reverenced. The woman of substance is not a lazy or poor woman. She is strong, wise and rich.

Proverb 31:14-18;

She is like the ships of traders. She brings her food from far away she gets up while it is still dark. She provides food for her family. She also gives some to her female servants she considers a field and buys it. She uses some of the money she earns to plant a vineyard she gets ready to work hard. Her arms are strong she sees that her trading earns a lot of money. Her lamp doesn't go out at night.

In Cameroon, we have what we call bush markets. These are markets where foodstuffs are sold considerably cheaper. The wise woman knows she does not have to misuse her finances even though she has enough and wakes up early enough, goes far off to bush markets so as to buy at cheaper prices in a bid to economize and save for rainy days ahead or to bless the work of God and the poor.

The modern woman minister of the gospel is a rounded woman. When it comes to the word of God, material, finance, education etc, she is balanced and rich and preaches the gospel without fear and compromise but with self-confidence and boldness.

❖ A dynamic woman

Judges 4:4-5

Deborah was a prophetess. She was the wife of Lappidoth. She was leading Israel at that time. Under the Palm Tree of Deborah she served the people as their judge. That place was between Ramah and Bethel in the hill country of Ephraim. The people of Israel came to her there. They came to have her decide cases for them. She settled matters between them.

A female minister ought to be dynamic: a woman who is full of energy, ambition, new ideas and the ability to multi task. Deborah was such a dynamic woman. Judges 4:4-14. She was not only a judge in Israel but she also had a palm plantation *Judges 4:5* which means she was a farmer and if she sold her palms or oil, then she equally did business. She was also a prophetess and a housewife at the same time.

Judges 4:6-10

Deborah sent for Barak. He was the son of Abinoam. Barak was from Kedesh in the land of Naphtali. Deborah said to Barak, "The Lord, the God of Israel, is giving you a command. He says, 'Go! Take 10,000 men from the tribes of Naphtali and Zebulun with you. Then lead the way to Mount Tabor. ⁷ will draw Sisera into a trap. He is the commander of Jabin's army. I will bring him, his chariots and his troops to the Kishon River. There I will hand him over to you.'"

⁸ Barak said to her, "If you go with me, I'll go. But if you don't go with me, I won't go."

⁹"All right," Deborah said. "I'll go with you. But because of the way you are doing this, you won't receive any honor. The Lord will hand Sisera over to a woman."

So Deborah went to Kedesh with Barak. There he sent for Zebulun and Naphtali. And 10,000 men followed him. Deborah also went with him.

Deborah was equally very courageous and a woman of faith. After Ehud died, even men like Barak were afraid to confront their oppressor (Sisera) but Deborah courageously and confidently took the challenge by agreeing to Barak`s proposal to go with him for she was confident that God was with her. She went right to the end and fulfilled her task perfectly.

The woman minister is a woman full of faith and boldness. She protects her family by exercising faith and confidence in God knowing that the God they are serving will see them through. Deborah's family and the entire nation could count on her at a time when the country was in a chaotic state.

❖ **A woman of dignity**

A woman of dignity is a woman who commands respect through her behaviour. She is serious, calm, self-controlled and worthy of respect. As a minister of Christ, the woman minister should:

❖ Not be given to gossips: *1 Timothy 3:11 "In the same way, the women[c] are to be worthy of respect, not malicious talkers but temperate and trustworthy in everything*
❖ Should be discrete and honest *1 Timothy 2:3-5 "This is good, and pleases God our Savior, ⁴ who wants all people to be saved and to come*

23

to a knowledge of the truth. ⁵ *For there is one God and one mediator between God and mankind, the man Christ Jesus".*

Proverbs 31:25 "She is clothed with strength and dignity; she can laugh at the days to come".

- ❖ Should be sober and faithful; **Titus 2:4, 1 Timothy 3:11, Colossians 3:18.**
- ❖ Should be wise and kind. **Proverb 31:26.**
- ❖ Should have concern for the welfare of others **proverb 31:20**
- ❖ Should be diligent in whatever she does **proverb 31:26-27**
- ❖ Should feed strangers and care for others and be a giver **Genesis 18:6, Proverbs 31:20, 1 Timothy 2:10, 5:10.**

All the above will cause those around her to sing her praises and be proud of her as the husband and children of the virtuous woman of *proverb 31.* The woman of dignity keeps her house neat and orderly, cares for the family's clothing, is submissive to her husband and raises up children in the fear of God. She is a gaper or intercessor.

1 Timothy 4:14, proverb 31:15, proverb 31:21, 1 Samuel 25:25-29

Chapter 3

WISDOM FOR BUILDING AND DESTROYING THE HOME
(Proverb 24:3a)

Let's take a look at some few biblical women of old that the bible exhorts us to copy if we desire to be called their daughters.

"For this is the way the holy women of the past who put their hope in God used to adorn themselves. They submitted themselves to their own husbands, ⁶ like Sarah, who obeyed Abraham and called him her lord. You are her daughters if you do what is right and do not give way to fear.

A. instruments for building the home

1. As Interlligent as Abigail: 1 Samuel 25

Vs 2-3 *"A certain man in Maon, who had property there at Carmel, was very wealthy. He had a thousand goats and three thousand sheep, which he was shearing in Carmel. ³ His name was Nabal and his wife's name was Abigail. She was <u>an intelligent and beautiful</u> woman, but her husband was surly and mean in his dealings—he was a Calebite"*

Married to a bad tempered and unfriendly man, Abigail was probably used to trying to calm the turmoil he created and redeem the harm he inflicted without quarrelling as the bible describes her as an intelligent woman in the above scripture. We shall examine the wisdom of Abigail from 1 *Sam. 25* and draw some lessons that will help us as women in building our homes.

1.1 Wisdom of good relations

1 Samuel 25:14 ⁴

One of the servants warned Nabal's wife Abigail. He said, "David sent some messengers from the desert to give his greetings to our master. But Nabal shouted at them and made fun of them.

For the home to be solid and secured, the woman as the home builder must establish and build good relationship with all those in and around it. Abigail won the hearts of people around her and shared a good relationship with them. She was not proud towards her servants as some women do today. She was not mean to them but made friends with them and built a level of confidence so that they would not hide anything from her. One of Nabal's servants revealed David's plan to her about wiping out Nabal's family. He was quite confident of Abigail's wisdom to help out with the situation. It was Nabal's fault but because in his mind he knew Nabal was a wicked man he decided to confide to his wife knowing she was capable of quenching David's anger. *Verse 17.* Nabal for sure had other wives but Abigail was the one who won the hearts of the servants.

What relationship do you share with the people around you? Have you won the hearts of your servants, children, husband, neighbours etc. so they can confidently confide in you? A home without a solid relationship as foundation is bound to scatter. Having bad relationship at home is an open door for the enemy to get in and destroy it. But for Abigail's wisdom of maintaining good relationship with her servants, Nabal's entire household would have been completely wiped out.

1.2. Wisdom of silence and amendment *1 Samuel 25:18-19*

¹⁸ Abigail didn't waste any time. She got 200 loaves of bread and two bottles of wine. The bottles were made out of animal skins. She got five sheep that were ready to be cooked. She got a bushel of grain that had been cooked. She got 100 raisin cakes. And she got 200 cakes of pressed *figs. She loaded all of it on the backs of donkeys. ¹⁹ Then she told her servants, "Go on ahead. I'll follow you." <u>But she didn't tell her husband Nabal about it.</u>*

The bible mentions in *Isaiah 30:15b that in quietness and confidence shall our strength be*. Abigail knew this word and remained calm and confident in God. Even after being aware of the atrocity her husband had committed, she did not mention a word to him but quickly devised a way to appease the king and she did not waste time in quarrelling or arguing with him as some women will do today but quickly did the right thing before trouble started. She prepared gifts and sent servants ahead to meet David and his troop and she equally set out without telling her husband for she knew how surly and mean he was. She knew what to tell him and when. She gave a double portion of what David demanded.

How and when do you approach your husband when you have a complaint against him? Do you make amends for the wrongs he commits or you instead expose him the more to the people he wrongs. Wise woman, use your talents and gifts to appease the heart of the king (Jesus) so his mercy will be shown on our families.

1.3 The wisdom of Humility *1 Samuel 25:23-24*

"Pride goes before destruction. A haughty spirit before a fall" Proverb 16:18

Abigail as said in *verse 3* was a very beautiful and intelligent woman who was married to a very rich man *1 Samuel 25:2* yet she never took pride in all these because she understood the above proverb.

"1 Samuel 25:23-24.

When Abigail saw David, she quickly got off her donkey and bowed down before David with her face to the ground. She fell at his feet and said "my lord let the blame be on me alone please". Let your servant speak to you--------------"

What discernment and intelligence! Remember at this time that David was not yet the king. He was fleeing from Saul and could barely eat with his servants. Abigail could discern God's plans for him as being the future king and humbled herself before him for God had chosen him. She was not a carnal woman and did not feel superior in her riches and was not mean to God's servant; instead she dropped down from her donkey and bowed to him despite his present condition of lack. Abagail's humility and intelligence finally landed her in the palace. What is your approach towards someone God has placed in authority? Are you mean to him/her because you feel you are wealthy or you show reference for God through his established authority? Humility is the gateway to greatness. Through humility, Abigail and Esther became queens.

1.4 Wisdom of intercession *1 Samuel 25:26-35*

"Sir, the LORD has kept you from killing Nabal and his men. He has kept you from using your own hands to get even. May what's about to happen to Nabal happen to all of your enemies. May it also happen to everyone who wants to harm you. And may it happen just as surely as the LORD and you are alive.

[27]"I've brought a gift for you. Give it to the men who follow you. [28]Please forgive me for what I've done wrong.

"The LORD will certainly give you and your family line a kingdom that will last. That's because you fight the LORD's battles. Don't do anything wrong as long as you live.

[29]"Someone may chase you and try to kill you. But the LORD your God will keep your life safe like a treasure that is hidden in a bag. And he'll destroy your enemies. Their lives will be thrown away, just as a stone is thrown from a sling.

[30]"The LORD will do for you every good thing he promised to do. He'll appoint you leader over Israel. [31]When that happens, you won't have this heavy load on your mind. You won't have to worry about how you killed people without any reason. You won't have to worry about how

you got even. The LORD will give you success. When that happens, please remember me."

[32]David said to Abigail, "Give praise to the LORD. He is the God of Israel. He has sent you today to find me. [33]May the LORD bless you for what you have done. You have shown a lot of good sense. You have kept me from killing Nabal and his men this very day. You have kept me from using my own hands to get even.

[34]"It's a good thing you came quickly to meet me. If you hadn't come, not one of Nabal's men would have been left alive by sunrise. And that's just as sure as the LORD, the God of Israel, is alive. He has kept me from harming you."

[35]Then David accepted from her what she had brought him. He said, "Go home in peace. I've heard your words. I'll do what you have asked."

Abigail's intercession saved both Nabal's family and stopped David from soiling his hands with blood. Our intercession can go as far as saving both our families and the nation and stop God's anger. The bible in speaking about the complacent women in Jerusalem in *Isaiah 32:9-20* says God's people can only live in peaceful dwelling places, in secured homes, in undisturbed places of rest *verses 18-20* if the complacent women awakes from their complacence, strip off their clothes, put on sack clothes round their waist and mourn for the land. Here, we see the power of a woman's intercession equally. As a woman just like Abigail did, let us stand in the gap between our families and the king (Jesus) interceding to the king on their behalf so that we can live in peaceful dwellings and secured homes.

"Consider now! Call for the wailing women to come; send for the most skilful of them. Let them come quickly and wail over us till our eyes overflow with tears and water streams from our eyelids". Jeremiah 9:17-18.

Each time there was problem, the lord asked for women through his prophets to wail. it is about time women wake from their places of ease and wail for their wilful husbands or children. Nabal never changed yet Abigail interceded for him. She played her part in doing the right thing.

God has placed us in the position to intercede and therefore let us do our part so that tomorrow we shall not be blamed or feel guilty.

Observe Abigail's words in *verse 27b "The Lord will certainly give you and your family line a kingdom that will last. That's because you fight the Lord's battles. Don't do anything wrong as long as you live.* Notice how her words coincides with *2 Sam. 7:16 "And your house and your kingdom shall be made sure forever before me. Your throne shall be established forever* "indicating she was a woman of the word. She knew God's prophetic promises to David and believed in them.

1.5 The wisdom of Right time of approach. *1 Samuel 25:36-38*

Abigail's approach caused Nabal great shock and dead. He could not imagine what she went through yet in silence so his heart failed. When she returned from appeasing the king, there was merriment in the house and knowing who her husband was she did not dare approach him at the time but waited till the following morning when he was sober (*verse 37*). Woman, when do you approach your husband or children each time they do wrong? People are different and therefore it is wise to understand the people around you so as to know what approach or method is suitable for each person you are dealing with.

2. As submissive as Sarah

To be submissive means to be meek and obedient. It is not easy to be the wife of a wanderer. Sarah was such yet she remained loyal and submissive to follow Abraham when God spoke to him saying "Get out of your country, from your family and from your father's land to a land that I will show you," she was so submissive that she even agreed to Abraham's deceit of King Abimelech *Genesis 20:2-7*. It was due to Sarah's submissiveness that even though not a perfect woman God had mercy on her at her old age and visited her and gave her Isaac. Meekness is a beauty that no man can resist no matter how difficult he might be. Abraham served God and fulfilled destiny in his days and became the father of faith partly because he had a submissive wife who went along with him. Her son Isaac crushed the head of the serpent in his generation by fathering the twelve great tribes of Israel who shook the kingdom of darkness represented by Egypt.

3. As determined and focused as Hannah and Jochebed

These women did not stay away from their children at their tender ages. They both had a common objective looking closely at their stories. They were determined to see their children crush the serpent's head and so they remained focused on that.

Proverbs 22:6

"Train a child in the way he should go and when he is old, he will not turn from it".

Hannah had made a vow unto the lord that Samuel will serve him all the days of his life *1 Samuel 1:11*. She dedicated herself in training him at his young age to serve God. The goal was so strong in her that she refused going to offer the annual sacrifice at Shiloh with the excuse that the child must be weaned first. *1 Samuel 1:21-23*. The weaning was not just physical but equally spiritual because after the mother let go of him, Samuel could stay in God's presence alone without being bored or afraid. He did not cling to his mother as children will often do. Remember the bible says he was very young at the time, *1samuel 1:24*. He knew Shiloh which represented God's presence at that time was the right place for him to be because his mom taught him so and released him at the appropriate time. That was not all. Hannah supported her son in the ministry to make sure he did not deviate. Each year, she made him a little robe and took it to him when she went up with her husband to offer the annual sacrifice. Samuel as we all know became a very great prophet and judge in Israel and the bible makes us to understand that none of his words ever fell to the ground *1 Samuel 3:9*

Jochebed on her part had three children who all crushed the head of the serpent (Aaron, Miriam and Moses). They all became mighty instruments in God's hands. When Moses, her last child was born, they were under severe hardship in Egypt. Every male child born to an Israelite at that time was forcefully thrown by the Egyptians as Pharaoh commanded but Jochebed could discern a divine destiny upon her son Moses. She hid him until when she could no longer hide him and then she made a papyrus basket for him and coated it with tar and pitch.

Exodus 2:2.

² She became pregnant and had a son by him. She saw that her baby was a fine child. So she hid him for three months.

She then put the basket into the water having faith in God that the water will carry him to his destiny. She had instructed her daughter (Miriam) to keep an eye on him so when Pharaoh's daughter through compassion took Moses, Miriam proposed to get a nurse who will help her out with the baby. It was therefore his real mother who became his nurse. She took her time and taught her son about the God of the Israelites.

Even though Moses had an Egyptian name and was considered the king's grandson, yet due to his mother's teachings he was not flattered by the luxurious and easy life in the palace. He knew through his mother's teachings that the king and the Egyptians were their enemies and was ready to crush them if the opportunity arose. He killed the Egyptian who was fighting with an Israelite and later faced his foster grandfather for war. He was a powerful weapon in God's hands and God used him to crush the serpent's head. Aaron his brother served the Lord throughout his life as a priest together with his sons, *Exodus 28:1*, *Numbers 18:1.* Miriam was a prophetess, who spoke God's word and as a praise and worship leader, she led the women of Israel in declaring his victory *Exodus 15:20-21*

These women knew why they existed and focused on it and the result was rewarding both for them and God.

B. INSTRUMENTS FOR DESTROYING THE HOME

Anything contrary to the above are instruments for destroying the home but there is a common one which I call the *"looking back syndrome"*. *Luke 17:32.* There is an obvious mistake which Lot's wife committed and that the word of God in a whole verse exhorts us to remember Lot's wife. Even after God had warned them not to turn and look back to Sodom as they were running away, Lot's wife stubbornly did look back and did not escape the consequence that followed.

"Looking back" can simply mean **"Lust"**. The looking back syndrome is very common among Christian women today and even though they profess to have become born again children of God yet their behaviour is not different from that of Lot's wife. Eve, the mother of humanity equally suffered from this syndrome and brought separation between God and men which only took the life of Jesus Christ for man to regain access to God. Lust pushed Eve to lead her entire household astray. *Genesis 3:6-19*. This is the more reason why women should constantly watch over their lives so as not to be swayed by the cares of this life. The syndrome of looking back has caused many Christian women to destroy their homes as their measuring tool for greatness or God's blessing in life is no longer on Godly principles but worldly standards and achievements. Many women push their husbands and children into making wrong decisions like Eve and this sometimes contributes in destroying the home.

Chapter 4

UNDERSTANDING FOR ESTABLISHMENT
(Proverb 24:3b)

"Understanding is a fountain of life to those who have it but folly brings punishment to fools" proverbs 16:22.

We can only be established in our homes, churches and societies if we understand those living with us. Abigail overcame her husband's folly, won the favor of King David all because she understood each of them and knew how and when to approach them. The bible says *"two cannot walk together except they agree"* **Amos 3:3.** Understanding those around us is a good and perfect breach to agreeing with them as we shall know exactly what motivates each person and the appropriate approach to use toward each individual so as to win them over.

In this chapter, we shall summarize the different types of persons with examples from the bible by using the four personality types.

Understanding people motivate them, help in effective communication, appreciate and tolerate the differences in them and improve relationship. Understanding people's temperament can help us become aware of which of their behaviour to encourage and which ones to avoid. If you know a person prefers gifts over word, you will know gifts will be his motivation over verbal complement.

No two persons are the same and therefore it becomes unreasonable and unwise when we compare our beloved ones with others. What motivates one person might not be applicable to another. God created every person unique, fearfully and wonderfully and for a unique purpose and therefore every person should be treated as such.

Psalms 139:14-17

"I will praise you for I am fearfully and wonderfully made. Marvellous are your works, and that my soul knows very well. My frame was not hidden from you when I was made in secret and skilfully wrought in the lowest parts of the earth. Your eyes saw my substance, being yet unformed. And in your book they all were written, the days fashioned for me when as yet there were none of them. How precious also are your thought to me, o God! How great is the sum of them.

SECTION A

In this section, we shall examine the three different types of children and what mothers can do in order to help their child excel in life. The child's development is greatly influenced by the adults in their lives. Children learn a lot by imitating what they see the elderly do. While using temperament to parent our children, we must always remember to use the right approach corresponding to the temperament. The following must be kept in mind when raising kids for we cannot successfully teach, nurture and guide if we do not know those we are childbearing and use the right method in approaching them.

We should know the child's temperament, know our temperament as well, always explain to the child the reason for certain actions and be a good role model.

a) The easy going children

Characteristics

These children are generally calm and friendly, happy, easy to deal with, regular in their sleeping or eating and quickly adapt to environmental changes. They are not easily upset and don't demand much from their parents.

Suggested approach

Such children simply demand attention and approval. Talk with them especially when seem to be disappointed or hurt because they won't talk about it on their own. This helps to strengthen relationship with them and also gives a better understanding of the children's likes, dislikes and the kind of person they are.

b. The Action children

Characteristics

These are children who are hyper active. Always engaged in doing something. Cannot be calm etc. They are not regular in sleeping and eating. They fear new people and situations and easily get upset by noise. They are intense in their reactions. They can for example express their frustration by throwing things.

Suggested approach: Fill their play areas with all sorts of toys to exercise their energy with some freedom of choice. Make changes around them regularly and try to direct them do and accept the right things

c. The timid children

Characteristics

These children are slow. They get to adapt and accept people and new environment gradually with time. They usually prefer to be in their usual environment or comfort zone.

Suggested approach

Do lots of repetition so as to help them get used to it. Equally give them enough time to get used to their environment and the people around them so as to help them come out of their world of fear.

A mother should often examine each of her children, observe and note the tendencies then adapt the right approach. That is the child's personality and uniqueness having its strength and weaknesses. Using the right approach will help the child develop into the person God wants him/her to be and help the child blossom in life.

Biblical Examples of different personalities and how God approached them

Studying the different kinds of people in the bible gives us examples of the different kinds of people we meet in our daily lives. Also, knowing how God approached them gives us ideas on how to approach people with like characteristics

Peter – The expressive

The apostle peter can be classified under the expressive personality type who are generally lovely, friendly, people pleasers and motivational. They are popularly known as the spice of the society. They are not firm and change very easily. They are very repentant people but will easily be over taken by sin. They are emotional which makes them very sensitive. We see Peter in the following passages expressing his emotional and unstable personality.

Matt. 26:33-35 But Peter said to Him, "Even though all may fall away because of You, I will never fall away. "Jesus said to him, "Truly I say to you that this very night, before a rooster crows, you will deny Me three times." Peter said to Him, "Even if I have to die with You, I will not deny You." All the disciples said the same thing too

He later changed and denied Jesus due to *t*hreats by a lay servant girl and wept after realizing he did not keep his promise to Jesus.

Having arrested Him, they led Him and brought Him into the high priest's house. But Peter followed at a distance. Now when they had kindled a fire in the midst of the courtyard and sat down together, Peter sat among them. And a certain servant girl, seeing him as he sat by the fire, looked intently at him and said, "This man was also with Him. "But he denied Him saying, "Woman, I do not know Him." And when he realized he had not kept his promise to Jesus, he wept

Approaching a peter

When approaching a peter, be sincere and focus on people as they are people lovers.. Because they are sensitive people, mine your body expression. Peters can be very productive when appreciated and encouraged with what they do without which they easily give up. Under the influence of the Holy Spirit, they love prayers, *(Acts 10 :19),* worship, and become very humble wise and discerning. Under pressure, Peter knew what to say. *(Acts 9:36-42) (Aacts 4:18-20)*

Paul – The goal getter

The goal getter is a man of enthusiasm; He does all it takes to get things done, and aspires after great things. He doesn't easily give up in the face of difficulties. The goal getter is very passionate and determined. He is a wall breaker. Whenever he is bent upon carrying out his plans or finds opposition, he is filled with passionate excitement and does not give up easily.

Paul was a man who was not afraid of persecution or imprisonment. He never did ordinary things. While the other Apostles were busy with maintaining and preaching the gospel to the Jews only, Paul went out to the gentiles and clearly said without fear that his ambition was to preach to the gentiles.

Romans 15:20 "It has always been my ambition to preach the gospel where Christ was not known, so that I would not be building on someone else's foundation".

Even when Agabus foretold what awaits Paul at Jerusalem,*(Acts 21: 1-26)* Paul was not dissuaded from going. Paul's many trials did not deter him from living a Christian life. Neither did they restrict him from preaching the gospel. To the contrary, suffering seemed to motivate him to even greater spiritual service. He said something remarkable about his adversities:

"For Christ's sake, I delight in weaknesses, in insults, in hardships, in persecutions, in difficulties. For when I am weak, then I am strong" (2 Corinthians 12:1

Approaching a Paul

When approaching Paul, go straight to the point and be precise. Pauls are busy people and do not have time to waste. To win them over, explain issues to them calmly and patiently. Never behave as though you know better than they do and avoid auguring

Apostle Paul was determined and focussed on God's call to the gentiles so much so that he lived his whole life for that. He says in *Philippians 1:21"*

"For to me, to live is Christ and to die is gain. But if I am to live on in the flesh, this will mean fruitful labour for me; and I do not know which to choose".

After God won Paul over to his side, he did not need to struggle to convince him but just strengthened and gave him all the assignments which Paul went ahead to accomplish with determination and fulfilment.

Moses – The Analyst

Analysts are generally intelligent, perfectionist, Self-sacrificing and loyal leaders. Moses chose to live by faith and to trust God Hebrew. 11:24-27. it was due to his loyalty that the journey to the Promised Land went successful. They are the right people when it comes to doing a task that needs sacrificing for other people. Moses because of his sacrificial character missed to enter the Promised Land. The Analyst easily feels inferior and depressed even though very talented. We see Moses even when he was called by God how he responded by trying to convince God that he was not the right person because he thought he knew nothing and that no one will believe him because he cannot speak well in public etc. Exodus 3:13, 4:1, 4:10. But when he took upon the task, he was just the right fit for it.

Approaching a Moses

Exodus 3:12

"So he said, I will certainly be with you. And this shall be a sign to you that I have sent you: When you have brought the people out of Egypt, you shall serve God on this mountain"

God's approach was not that of criticism but of reassurance and encouragement. He promised he will be with him because he knew Moses could carry out the task. He had anointed and gifted him for it but he only needed to be reassured and encouraged.

It only takes reassurance and encouragement for Moses' to accomplish their tasks. They don't need fearful or negative people around them else they go back into their depressing state. Moses' should be accompanied by Aarons, Hurs and Joshuas and they'll effectively carry out their tasks with great success.

Abraham – The Amiable: Generally calm, peacemakers, Dependable, and Cautious people. They are the easiest people in the world to get along with but the least motivated. They make great leaders when they accept to but never volunteer to be one.

Abraham, our crowned father of faith was willing to go as God led. Once God said then he believed he would do. Once he promised he had faith he'd fulfil. Hebrew 11:6, Genesis 22:8. Amiables are very neutral kind of people. We see how Abraham gave up his wife to king Abimelech so easily. Genesis 20:1-2

And Abraham journeyed from thence toward the south country, and dwelled between Kadesh and Shur, and sojourned in Gerar. And

Abraham said of Sarah his wife, she is my sister: and Abimelech king of Gerar sent, and took Sarah. And later in Gen. 22:1-19, once God instructed, he took his son Isaac for sacrifice.

Approaching Abraham

The Amiable will scarcely rise up on their own to do something due to their lack of motivation and their care free attitude. They constantly need very patient people because they are full of complaints. Wives of this type ought to be very patient because they are the most henpecked husbands. God never struggled much with Abraham on obedience but only he had to stand and defend him before king Abimelech. Most wives of this types are their defenders and motivators. Because they will do all just to maintain peace even against their wish, they need people sometimes to stand and defend their rights.

41

Chapter 5

KNOWLEDGE FOR BEAUTY

"Through knowledge its rooms are filled with rare and beautiful treasures" Proverb 24:4

In this chapter we shall basically be examining some of the practical lessons we give at the wisdom for women training centre. Beauty is defined both internally and externally and this is what we shall dwell on. This internal and external beauty made up of our interior character and physical presentation is both taught and acquired. We cannot do or give what we do not know.

How, then, can they call on the one they have not believed in? And how can they believe in the one of whom they have not heard? And how can they hear without someone preaching to them? Rom 10:14

We equally cannot know without learning. We must know God's word in order to define Christian beauty and we must learn in order to know how to tidy and decorate our homes, bodies, and churches etc. The Bible says **"My people perish for lack of knowledge"** *Hosea 4:6.* We must be willing to acquire knowledge. It is never too late to learn, therefore let's seize any opportunity which comes our way.

Part A. Internal beauty

This consists of the interior made up of one's behavioural character and morals. This is acquired from various backgrounds where we spring from.

Some of these behaviours are subjective to the society from where we grow while others are generally acceptable good behaviour. As Christians, any behaviour we put up that contradicts the word of God is out of question of being a good one. The bible is clear in **proverbs 31:30**

"Charm is deceitful and beauty is passing but a woman who fears the lord shall be praised".

The beauty the bible mentions here as passing is physical. The bible goes further to talk about internal beauty in *1 Peter 3V3 – 6*

"Do not let your adornment be merely outward putting on fine apparels rather let it be the hidden person of the heart, with the incorruptible beauty of a gentle and quiet spirit which is very precious in the sight of God. For in this manner in former times, the holy women who trusted in God also adorned themselves, being submissive to their husbands as Sarah obeyed Abraham, calling him lord, whose daughters you are if you do good and are not afraid with any terror".

The bible from the above scripture gives two clear characteristics of an internal beauty

- **Incorruptible beauty of a gentle and quiet spirit**

Here, the Bible does not speak of the kind of quietness generally known as **"slow water runs deep".** Not the kind that outwardly a person is quiet with bitterness, hypocrisy and murmuring being the main drive behind. It speaks of an incorruptible beauty of a gentle and quiet spirit. This speaks of transparency, not compromising with sin and that gives peace and tranquillity to one's spirit. That is to say, ones spirit can testify that he/she is at peace with both men and God through the internal calmness that it experiences.

- **Submission**

Like we have already seen in chapter one, women ought to be submissive to their husbands and even be good examples of submission to established authorities. Below is a perfect example from the book of Esther.

The Beautiful Esther

Here, we shall examine Esther's secret beauty that made her win the favour of the people around her and even the king:

"Now when the time came for Esther the daughter of Abigail the uncle of Modecia who had taken her as his daughter to go into the king, she requested nothing but what Hagai the king's eunuch, the custodian of the women, advised. And Esther obtained favour in the sight of all who saw her" Esther 2v15

Esther did not just get up one day and decided on her own volition to contest for the vacant position of a queen. She went through some processes and came to a place where she won the favour of men.

1) Knowledge in obedience:

Favour begins at home. Esther was greatly loved by Mordecai with whom she grew up and who assumed the duty of her father. She found favour with him because she was obedient. She first of all obtained favour from her father's home and he pushed her into the next level and gave her the secret necessary for that level "**discretion**"

Esther 2:10. **"Esther had not revealed her nationality and family background, because Mordecai had forbidden her to do so".**

This was the knowledge given to her before she left home, otherwise she would have messed up herself. Esther sealed her mouth and remained silent in the palace. That was to be the secret of her success at that level or she would have been eliminated. She planned to complain to the king about Haman, plotted her plans alone until the appointed time when she was certain it was the right time to speak. We ought to be careful with curiosity. There is knowledge that is revealed only through obedience. The bible says Obedience is better than sacrifice. Abraham came to the knowledge and plans of God about the destruction of Sodom and Gomorrah because he was obedient. He even gained his fame as our father of faith through obedience.

The beauty in Discretion and Obedience (Esther 2:8-9)

"so it was, when the king's command and decree were head, and when many young women were gathered at shushan the citadel, under the custody of Hegai, that Esther also was taken to the king's palace, in the care of Hegai the custodian of the women, now the young woman pleased him, and she obtained his favour, so he readily gave beauty preparations to her, besides her allowance. The seven choice maidservants were provided for her from the king's palace, and he moved her and her maidservants to the best place in the house of the women"

It is clear from the above passage that Esther won the heart of Hegai who held the secret into the heart of the king. The king did not choose Esther because she was the most physically beautiful. All the girls chosen for the context were all beautiful as the passage describes. She had the secret into the king's heart. Favour is usually won from character which Esther had acquired from her background. In the palace it is certain that through her obedience and discreet nature, Hegai found in her the quality of a queen and decided to reveal to her the secret into the king's heart. She was even separated from the others and moved to the best place in the house of the women.

2) The Knowledge of fasting and prayer

Fasting and prayers are weapons that not even the strongest king would resist. God himself will not resist the fasting and prayers of the righteous and what more of lay humans. It is a privilege for us children of God having this knowledge as weapon, knowing that we can move mountains and even the strongest demon from our way to success through fasting and prayers.

"Go, gather all the Jews who are present in Shushan, and fast for me. Neither eat nor drink for three days night or day. My maids and I will fast likewise and so I will go to the king which is against the law and if I perish I perish ". Esther 4v16

"Now, it happened on the third day that Esther put on her royal robes and stood in the inner court of the king's palace, across from the king's house while the king sat on his royal throne in the royal house, facing

the entrance of the house. So it was, when the king saw Queen Esther standing in the court, which she found favor in his sight, and the king held out to Esther the golden sceptre that was in his hand. Then Esther went near and touched the top of the sceptre and the king said to her what do you wish Queen Esther? What is your request? It shall be given to you up to half the kingdom!". Esther "5v1-3

The above scripture in which Esther obtained great favour before the king and answer to her prayers was the result of the fasting and prayers in chapter 4 v16. Fasting and prayers is one of the greatest internal beauties that can pull down obstacles in our lives and transcend any law. Haman was a great obstacle in the lives of the people of Israel. Through Esther's suggestion of fasting and prayers, Haman was pulled down and his evil plans exposed which raised the Jews to an elevated position in shushan and transcended the law that any man or woman who went into the inner court of the king who had not been called was to be put to death except the king held out the golden sceptre. Esther took the risk saying she would go to the king which was against the law and if she perished she perished. She was submissive, discreet, clothed with a quiet and gentle spirit, determined and was prayerful which raised her to the position of a queen and brought her people to a high position of honour in Shushan.

PART B External Beauty (Esther 2:2-3)

"Then the king's servants who attended him said: Let beautiful young virgins be sought for the king; and let the king appoint officers in all the provinces of his kingdom, that they may gather all the beautiful young virgins to Shushan the citadel, into the women's quarters, under the custody of Hegai the king's eunuch, custodian of the women.

Although charm is deceitful and physical beauty passing as the Bible puts it in *Proverbs 31: 30,* the physique is the first aspect that attracts. No man will want to get a woman who is not physically attractive. The woman is the man's pride and therefore he won't want to get a wife he can't be proud of. It is the physical that pulls the man first and then the internal follows. Only the physically beautiful virgins were chosen to be taken to the palace for this contest. If Esther was not first of all physically a beautiful virgin she would not have qualified for this position. After she qualified for the physical while in the palace, the internal made her win the contest.

The bible says God created all beautiful so the question is what makes us look physically ugly? The simple answer is the way we treat our bodies. Some women neglect themselves to the extent that even their body odour can scare people from them. Physical attractiveness is comprised of our Physical appearance and abilities. The virtuous woman of **Proverbs 31** was such a woman. She feared God, yet she kept her home and family physically attractive.

Proverbs 31. 21-27

"When it snows she has no fear for her household; for all of them are clothed in scarlet. She makes coverings for her beds; she is clothed in fine linen and .... Vs26 She opens her mouth with wisdom and on her tongue is the law of knowledge vs 27She watches over the affairs of her house hold "and does not eat the bread of idleness".

The wise woman watches over the affairs of her household. Always busy making sure everything is in its rightful place. She clothes herself in fine linen and controls her tongue.

At the wisdom for women Centre, external beauty includes home keeping and personal hygiene. Home keeping is the physical beauty and organization of the house and the ability to cook good meal. In personal hygiene, we reveal tips that can make a woman have an appealing appearance. All these are the knowledge the woman needs for rare and beautiful treasures. Subjects in home keeping include internal decoration of the home, sewing, cooking of national dishes, cakes, fruit juices, salads etc and intensive cleaning of the house. While personal hygiene includes subjects like hairdressing, and general body care. Being aware that not all women can be able to take lessons from our centres due to lack of time, we organize yearly conferences where some of our lessons are given so that we can reach a maximum number of women.

Some unethical behaviours and appearances that affect our physical beauty

- Picking nose in the public

- Leaning behind the chair of an elderly person

- Stretching out hands firsts to greet an elderly person (depending on the society in which we are)

- Receiving phone calls while conversing with an authority figure or without excusing yourself.

- Interrupting people conversing without asking for permission

- Eavesdropping

- Leaving the table without reason while others are still eating

- Being inattentive or distracted while conversing with someone

- Chewing while conversing with an authority

- Taking sit in someone's office or home without being asked to

- Shouting and calling someone's name in public

- Demonstrating ungratefulness

- Being sarcastic or impolite

- Being provocative

- Sneezing or yawning in public with open month

- Frowning faces or putting up attitudes.

- Not admitting fault

- Being defensive etc

- Changing the body colour

- Having bad body and mouth odor

THE WOMAN'S PRAYER

Father, I come to you in the name of our Lord and Saviour Jesus Christ to present my life as a woman.

You said in *Psalms 50:1 "Call on me in the day of trouble and I will deliver you".*

I present the home, church, and society in which you have made me mother, wife, and minister and I pray that you will deliver me from all those weaknesses in my life that contribute in destroying my home and ministry.

In the name of Jesus, I come against any spiritual blindness that hinders me from seeing and accepting my role as a woman or any inferiority complex of my sex.

I neutralize the power of any haughty spirit making me to be proud and unwilling to learn.

By the blood of Jesus, I neutralize any looking back syndrome in my life and I run to the name of Jesus the strong tower through which the righteous are saved.

By faith, I declare that I am free from Satan's deceptions and I accept my place of a woman in the name of Jesus.

Father you say in *Proverbs 14:1* that it is the wise woman who builds her home.

Proverb 1:7 also records that the fear of the lord is the beginning of wisdom.

Grant to me the spirit to fear and obey you so that I will be wise and I will build my home according to the divine pattern.

I therefore pray that in wisdom I will effectively carry out my responsibilities as a wife by being a perfect help for (Husband' name).

Father Help me to recognize and appreciate the great intuition you have put within the woman, and grant that I will use it for your glory alone.

Open my eyes lord to be able to discern (husband's name) portion in the garden and to help him in tending and tilling it as you had purposed from the beginning.

I pray father that I will be a source of encouragement to him in tending and tilling our own portion in the garden and not one that gets in the way or one that stands as a hindrance rather than a help.

I pray lord that I will be prompt in supporting (name) in the area of his need.

Apart from being effective in home-making, grant lord that I will take interest in (name) work and hobbies.

Father, grant that I will be a good listener, peacemaker and that I will show respect for (name). Also that I will be sympathetic and compassionate towards him during challenging moments.

I pray lord that you will help me to be like Abigail in 1 *Samuel 25* who built good relationships with her servants and all those around her despite her social status.

Father, grant me the grace to build good relationships around me without considering the social statuses of people.

Also like Abigail, give me the wisdom of silence and amendment as in *1 Samuel 25:18-19,* so that in silence, I will calm any chaos my husband or children may create and redeem any harm they inflict without complaining.

I pray I will be noted before you for being humble before all authorities you have established so that my family will experience forgiveness through my humility just like Nabal's through Abigail's humility.

In the name of Jesus, I decree that I shall constantly and tirelessly stand in the gap on behalf of my family. Thank you father for the grace to be patient and approach (name of husband) only at the right time when his mind and senses are in their right state of receiving reproach and advice.

Father, like Sarah was submissive to Abraham, I pray that my beauty will not consist of the physical apparels I wear but submission will be my emblem in the name of Jesus.

Lord, in my role of a mother- as teacher, nurturer and guide, I pray that you will give me the virtues of patience, perseverance and hope, trusting and depending on you like Jochebed and Hannah for the proper upbringing of my children.

Grant Lord that I will be determined and focused as these women.

Put Lord a craving desire in my heart not to just stay around my children, but to wean them at the appropriate time like Hannah weaned Samuel and also impact their lives through training and teaching them the right, Godly and moral societal norms and principles.

I pray Father that just like Hannah taught Samuel that the presence of the lord was the best place to be, may you grant me that ability to teach my children the importance of your presence and to be a role model for them.

Father, may my children crush the head of the serpent like Jodchebed's children did. I pray lord that (cite names of children) will be mighty instruments in your hands in the name of Jesus.

Just like Jochebed could discern the destiny of her son Moses and protected him from Pharaoh's wicked decree, I pray that I too will discern the destinies of (names of children) and also protect them from any wicked plan of Pharaoh.

I therefore come against any Pharaoh in the lives of (names of children) and I decree that the waters will carry them to their destinies like the water carried Moses to his destiny in the name of Jesus.

As children are like mighty arrows in the hands of a warrior, I decree that (names of children) will be mighty arrows in your hands in the name of Jesus.

I decree that the present generation will not influence and turn them away from my teachings in the name of Jesus.

I decree that the fear and love of God will scare them from doing evil in the name of Jesus.

O God, that just like Jesus grew up in wisdom and stature and in favour with God and men, I decree that (name of children) will grow up in wisdom in every aspect of life in the name of Jesus.

That they will find favour before you, their teachers, their friends and anyone they get connected to.

I decree father that they will grow up in stature and crush the head of the serpent in their generation in the name of Jesus.

That you will connect them only to men who will connect them to their destinies.

By the blood of Jesus, I cancel any connection orchestrated by the devil in the name of Jesus.

Father, hold my hands and lead me through the path of wisdom. Grant me the privilege of being a model Christian woman in my home, neighbourhood, church and my community.

Give me the grace Lord to surpass my weaknesses with calmness, seriousness in all I do, self-control and behaviour that is worthy of respect.

By the blood of Jesus and the word of my testimony, I overcome gossip, disorderliness, dirtiness, pride, inferiority or superiority complexes, feelings of rejection, prayerlessness, carelessness, worldliness, laziness, self-centeredness, lavishness, poverty and any other weakness that wants to suppress the gifts and abilities God has invested in me.

Father, I pray that as your representative in my surrounding, you will fill me with substance, dignity, dynamism and a spirit of intercession.

Therefore, I pray and clothe myself with honesty, faithfulness, wisdom, kindness, diligence, meekness, orderliness, submissiveness, hospitality, cleanliness, concern for others and strength.

I pray father that you will grant me the grace to not allow the world define my womanhood but that I will know your call and the capacity you have put within me, explore and enjoy every opportunity you have set before me while being submissive to you, my husband and any authority you have established over me.

Grant me the grace to create a Godly atmosphere around me, be as bold and courageous as Deborah and as hard working and wise as the virtuous woman.

Above all else Lord, may I be completely soaked and overflowing by the Holy Spirit, may the fear and the word of God be my guide and may Jesus be the song that I sing forever and ever in the name of Jesus. AMEN.

The Woman's Hymn

I am a wise woman cause I hope in God

Lord help me build my home

God the father the son and the Holy Ghost

Please guide and lead me through.

Lord I need wisdom; to build my home
I need understanding; to be established Give me the knowledge; for rare and beautiful treasures (2*)"

CONCLUSION

The model woman in the Bible is the virtuous woman of *Proverbs 31*. She builds her home in wisdom, understands people around her environment in order to be established and does all to acquire necessary knowledge for rare and beautiful treasures. Above all, she is God fearing.

Having read the words of the pages of this book is not by chance. It is never too late. You can begin all over again. God is a father who gives opportunity to all. God is about to begin a new work in your life. Forget about the past and behold the promising future God has for you.

REFERENCES

- The Holy Bible

- http://sedevacantist.com/misc/temperaments.html

- http://www.psychoheresy-aware.org/images/4temp

Printed in the United States
By Bookmasters